Courageous Heroes
of the American West

Brigham Young
Courageous Mormon Leader

William R. Sanford and Carl R. Green

Enslow Publishers, Inc.
40 Industrial Road
Box 398
Berkeley Heights, NJ 07922
USA

http://www.enslow.com

Original edition published as *Brigham Young: Pioneer and Mormon Leader* in 1996.

Library of Congress Cataloging-in-Publication Data

Sanford, William R. (William Reynolds), 1927–
  Brigham Young : courageous Mormon leader / William R. Sanford and Carl R. Green.
     p. cm. — (Courageous heroes of the American West)
  Summary: "Examines Brigham Young, including his childhood and early life, becoming the
leader of the Mormon Church, leading his followers to the Great Salt Lake, his family, and his
legacy as an American pioneer"—Provided by publisher.
  Includes index.
  ISBN 978-0-7660-4004-5
  1. Young, Brigham, 1801–1877—Juvenile literature. 2. Church of Jesus Christ of Latter-day
Saints—Presidents—Biography—Juvenile literature. I. Green, Carl R. II. Title.
  BX8695.Y7S26 2013
  289.3092—dc23
  [B]

                                        2011031051

Future editions:
Paperback ISBN 978-1-4644-0089-6
ePUB ISBN 978-1-4645-0996-4
PDF ISBN 978-1-4646-0996-1

Printed in the United States of America

032012 Lake Book Manufacturing, Inc., Melrose Park, IL

10 9 8 7 6 5 4 3 2 1

To Our Readers: We have done our best to make sure all Internet addresses in this book were active
and appropriate when we went to press. However, the author and the publisher have no control over,
and assume no liability for, the material available on those Internet sites or on other Web sites they
may link to. Any comments or suggestions can be sent by e-mail to comments@enslow.com or to
the address on the back cover.

♻ Enslow Publishers, Inc., is committed to printing our books on recycled paper. The paper in
every book contains 10% to 30% post-consumer waste (PCW). The cover board on the outside of each
book contains 100% PCW. Our goal is to do our part to help young people and the environment too!

Illustration Credits: Brigham Young University Museum of Art, gift of the Christensen
Grandchildren, pp. 16, 25; Brigham Young University, Harold B. Lee Library, p. 42; Enslow
Publishers, Inc., p. 37; © Enslow Publishers, Inc. / Paul Daly, p. 1; The Granger Collection, NYC,
p. 33; Library of Congress Prints and Photographs, pp. 6, 12, 19, 21; © North Wind Picture
Archives, p. 28; Public Domain Image, p. 8.

Cover Illustration: © Enslow Publishers, Inc. / Paul Daly.

Contents

Authors' Note

This book tells the story of one of the Wild West's most unusual heroes. As a pioneering leader of the Mormon Church, Brigham Young had to be a preacher, farmer, builder, statesman, and family man. As you will learn, he excelled in all of these tasks. Because his ideas and actions aroused strong feelings among both Mormons and non-Mormons, reports of his activities filled the newspapers of the day. As often happened in the 1800s, some of the stories stretched the truth. All of the events described in this book actually happened.

Chapter 1

A Nearly Bloodless War

In July 1857, the Mormon settlers of Utah Territory awoke to a new threat. The United States was sending troops to install a new governor. Would they be forced to flee once again? They turned to Governor Brigham Young for guidance. Ten years before, Brigham had led them to their new home beside the Great Salt Lake.

Brigham knew that the Mormons and their church, the Church of Jesus Christ of Latter-day Saints, had few friends in Washington, D.C. Senator Stephen A. Douglas of Illinois was leading the attack. Douglas called the Mormon way of life a "cancer . . . gnawing into the very vitals of the [American] body politic."

President James Buchanan had his own reasons for sending troops. The slavery issue divided the nation.

This portrait of Brigham Young was taken sometime between 1855 and 1865.

An attack on the Mormons might turn attention away from that fierce debate.

Out in Salt Lake City, Brigham weighed his options. On his desk lay an offer of 30 million acres in Central America. To the north lay Canada and Alaska. The army, however, would arrive before his people could move. So, early in August, Brigham announced, "We have transgressed no law . . . as for any nation coming to destroy this people, God Almighty being my helper, it shall not be."

Workmen built forts at the entry points to the Salt Lake Valley. To slow the advancing troops, Brigham sent soldiers to cut off their supply line. The raiders burned three wagon trains and drove off a number of horses. They also burned two outposts. The raids, combined with early snowfalls, finished the job. The advancing troops were forced to set up winter camp in Wyoming.

When shooting did break out, it had nothing to do with Brigham. A party of settlers bound for California had reached southern Utah that same month. Riding with the wagon train was a band of horsemen known as the Missouri Wildcats. A local tribe of American Indians—the Ute—blamed the Wildcats for poisoning their wells. Mormons were equally outraged. Back in Illinois, the Wildcats bragged, they had helped kill the church's founder, Joseph Smith.

In southern Utah, Mormon and Ute hotheads planned revenge. Unsure of what to do, church elders sent word to Brigham. A rider covered the 250 miles to Salt Lake City in three days. Brigham replied at once. His orders read: "You must not meddle with them [the settlers]. . . . The Indians we expect will do as they please."

In 1857, Brigham Young sent word to his Mormon followers not to attack a wagon train headed for California. His dispatch, however, arrived too late. This illustration depicts the Mountain Meadows massacre, in which a force of Mormons and Ute warriors killed 120 settlers.

The dispatch arrived too late. On September 11, a force of Mormons and Ute warriors attacked the wagon train. When the Mountain Meadows massacre ended, 120 men, women, and children lay dead. Only seventeen small children survived. Brigham wept when he heard the terrible news. Did he know the depth of his militia's involvement? No one knows. To protect his people, he laid the blame on the Ute. The full truth did not emerge until years later.

The threat of invasion still haunted Brigham. As the winter wore on, he changed his tactics. First, he ordered his militia to end its attacks on the army's supply lines. Then he offered to step aside in favor of President Buchanan's choice as governor. Alfred Cumming agreed to enter Utah without an army escort. He reached Salt Lake City in April 1858.

In June, President Buchanan announced a full pardon for all Mormons. For his part, Brigham said the army could march through Salt Lake City. That act fulfilled the president's orders to "occupy" Mormon lands. As a safeguard, Brigham ordered Mormons to leave the city. Only a few trusted men stayed behind. They had orders to burn the city if the army set up a base there.

On June 26, the troops passed through a nearly silent city. To the south, thousands of Mormons waited and prayed. To their joy, the troops turned south to Cedar Valley. With the threat past, the settlers returned to their homes and farms.

In July, Brigham announced that the Utah War was over. It was one more triumph in a long and active life.

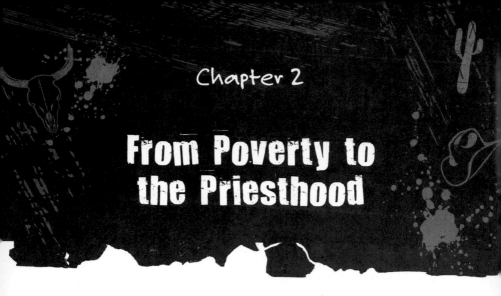

Chapter 2

From Poverty to the Priesthood

John Young served in George Washington's army during the American Revolution. After the war, he married Nabby Howe. By 1800, Nabby had given birth to five daughters and three sons. When his farm in upstate New York failed, John bought land in Whitingham, Vermont. Six months later, on June 1, 1801, Nabby gave birth to the Youngs' ninth child. They named the boy Brigham.

Vermont's rocky soil defeated John's best efforts. He and his older sons had to work as hired hands to pay their debts. The girls wove and sold straw hats. To make bad times worse, Nabby fell ill with tuberculosis. The work of raising Brigham and the younger children fell to Fanny, their fourteen-year-old sister.

In 1804, John bought virgin land near Smyrna, New York. He labored hard for weeks to clear the land for planting. As soon as he was old enough, Brigham took over his share of the chores. Money was in short supply. Later, Brigham recalled, "If I had on a pair of pants that would cover me I did pretty well."

The Smyrna farm failed, too. In January 1814, the Youngs moved fifty miles farther west. There was little money for schooling. Brigham later said he spent only eleven days in a classroom. His mother taught him to read and write. He spent his spare time hunting and fishing to help feed the family. Sundays were reserved for worship. As strict Methodists, the Youngs were not allowed to dance or listen to fiddle music.

Brigham's mother died in June 1815. With his older sisters married, Brigham was saddled with household duties. He baked bread, churned butter, and washed dishes. In 1817, John Young married a widow with several children. There was little room for Brigham in the new household. John told his sixteen-year-old son, "You can now have your time; go and provide for yourself."

For the next five years, Brigham lived in Auburn, New York. He turned his back on farming and found work with a furniture maker. The apprentice developed into a skilled woodworker. In 1823, Brigham moved to Port Byron. The town lay on the new Erie Canal.

A preacher, Samuel Smith, showed Brigham the Book of Mormon. Samuel explained that his brother, Joseph, had translated the book from a set of golden tablets. In this illustration, the angel Moroni descends to earth to deliver the tablets to Joseph Smith.

He repaired chairs, made pails and buckets, and worked in a boatyard.

Shop owners liked Brigham's steady work habits. The young women of the town liked his looks. The slender youth had matured into a sturdy, broad-chested young man. He stood five feet, ten inches tall, and looked at the world through clear blue eyes.

A local girl named Miriam Works fell in love with Brigham. They were married in October 1824.

Four years later, Brigham and Miriam moved with their baby daughter west to Mendon, New York. Brigham set up his own carpentry shop. Life seemed good. Then Miriam, too, fell prey to tuberculosis. Brigham had to neglect his work to care for her.

Brigham's hard life took a sudden turn in April 1830. A preacher named Samuel Smith showed him the *Book of Mormon*. It was a sacred book, Smith said, a supplement to the Bible. He explained that his brother Joseph had translated it from a set of golden plates. It told of a people who long ago left the Middle East. Their travels led them to the New World. These early settlers, he said, were the ancestors of the American Indians.

Brigham was impressed. He set himself the task of learning more about the Mormon Church. In January 1832, he visited a Mormon colony in Pennsylvania. What he saw there erased his doubts. On April 15, a church elder baptized Brigham in the stream behind his Mendon workshop.

The convert's clothes were still wet when the elder ordained him as a priest. Brigham preached his first sermon a week later.

Chapter 3

"Our Motto Is Go Ahead"

Brigham gave himself heart and soul to his new duties. The church sent him to travel across western New York as a missionary. He had little money, but needed little. His converts supplied him with food and shelter.

The last months of 1832 brought both joy and sorrow. The joy came when Brigham was introduced to Joseph Smith. Brigham felt that he was shaking the hand of the Prophet of God. The sorrow came that fall, when Miriam died. Certain that he would meet her in heaven, Brigham buried himself in his work.

In 1833, Brigham moved to Kirtland, Ohio. Smith had founded the town two years earlier. Brigham rolled up his sleeves and built homes for new converts. He also courted thirty-year-old Mary Ann Angell. Mary Ann saw in Brigham the "man of God" she had longed to meet. They married in February 1834.

The new church soon ran into trouble. Close-knit Mormon communities often took control of county politics. Non-Mormons felt frozen out. In Jackson County, Missouri, neighbors disliked the Mormons for not owning slaves. Others condemned the new religion. In November 1833, rampaging mobs drove a thousand Mormons from their homes.

Smith sent a force called Zion's Camp to aid the refugees. Brigham was one of the 205 men who made the nine-hundred-mile journey. During the day, he walked beside his wagon. At night, he slept on the hard ground. He reported that "they supplied musketos [mosquitoes] in that country, as they did eggs, by the bushel. . . ."

The only battle was broken up by a violent hail-storm. The fourteen men who died were killed by cholera, not bullets. They gave their lives in vain. Local officials turned a blind eye to the injustice. The Mormons never did regain their homes.

In 1835, Smith chose Brigham as one of his church's twelve apostles. The prophet ordered the Twelve to carry the word to all nations. For three years, Brigham preached in the eastern states. During his stays in Kirtland, he designed and installed

In this painting, violent mobs drive the Mormons out of their homes in Jackson County, Missouri. The attack was triggered by a growing distrust of the new religion.

windows in the new temple. His family was growing, too. Mary Ann gave birth to two sons and a daughter.

A new round of mob fury struck Kirtland late in 1837. It was triggered by the collapse of the Kirtland Safety Society. The wildcat bank had been Joseph Smith's pet project. Beset by debts, Smith sold off church property. Then he led his people to a fresh start in northwest Missouri. Brigham was one of three Senior Apostles who helped direct the move.

More than eight thousand Mormons already lived in Far West, Missouri. As the Mormons from Kirtland flooded in, fears of Mormon influence flared afresh.

Roving mobs burned Mormon homes and farms. Men from both sides died in pitched battles. As the unrest spread, Governor Lilburn Boggs spoke out. "The Mormons must be . . . driven from the state," he said in October 1838. Boggs's militia marched to Far West and arrested Smith. Hoping to prevent violence, the prophet did not resist. His efforts failed. The troops poured in and looted the town.

From his cell, Smith placed Brigham in charge of the church. Brigham and his family left Missouri early in 1839 to avoid arrest. By then he had organized the move of more than twelve thousand Mormons to Quincy, Illinois. In April, Smith escaped from jail. When he reached Quincy, he called on Mormons to build a new gathering place. Nauvoo (the beautiful place) quickly took root upriver from Quincy. A young legislator named Abraham Lincoln helped the city obtain its charter.

As Nauvoo grew, Brigham set off to preach in England. He arrived there in April 1840, seasick and nearly broke. English Mormons welcomed him with open arms. Soon, hundreds of converts were sailing for America. In a letter to Smith, Brigham explained his success: "Our motto is *go ahead*. Go ahead—and *ahead*."

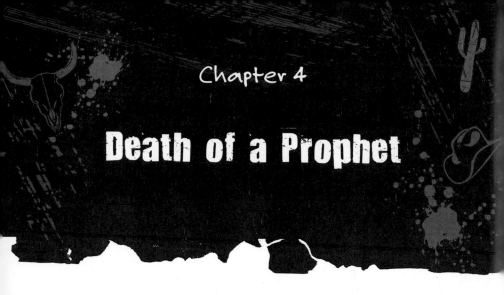

Chapter 4

Death of a Prophet

Brigham returned to Nauvoo from England in 1841. He found his family housed in a damp cabin. He set to work at once to drain and fence the swampy land. Then he built a brick storage cellar and a cowshed. It was the church, however, that claimed most of his time.

Joseph Smith revealed new doctrines to Brigham that fall. One offered baptism to the ancestors of living Mormons. The second exposed the church to years of conflict. It was God's will, Smith said, that Mormons should practice plural marriage. Taking many wives, he explained, would return the church to biblical traditions. Smith tried to keep the doctrine a secret, but reports leaked out.

The news added fuel to anti-Mormon feeling. Nauvoo's neighbors already disliked the Mormon practice of bloc voting. They also worried about the

During a tour of eastern cities, Brigham Young's sermons raised money for the Mormon temple that Joseph Smith was building in Nauvoo, Illinois. This drawing shows the place of worship that Brigham's preaching helped create.

new Mormon militia. Smith had formed the Nauvoo Legion to defend against mob attacks. Across the state, only a handful of leaders spoke up for the Mormons.

Brigham had a busy year in 1842. He saw his oldest daughter married, he welcomed a new baby, and married his first plural wife. In the fall, he toured the eastern states again. His sermons raised money to help build the Nauvoo temple. That winter, he nearly died of scarlet fever. By the spring of 1843, he was ready to begin work on a two-story brick home. He also married four more wives.

In March 1844, Smith told the Twelve that he would die soon. Then he announced a plan to run for president of the United States. Running, he said, would publicize the church and its beliefs. Brigham helped recruit three hundred volunteers to campaign for "the smartest man in the Union."

In nearby Carthage, anti-Mormon feeling ran high. A Carthage judge charged Smith with starting a riot. Smith allowed himself and his brother to be jailed. On June 27, an angry mob broke into the jail. The guards looked the other way. When the mob left, Joseph and Hyrum Smith lay dead.

After hearing news of the double murder, the Twelve gathered in Nauvoo. On August 8, the church's

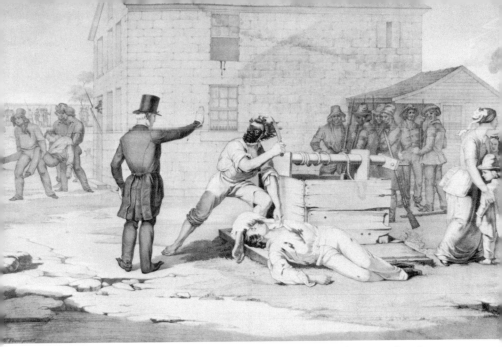

Joseph Smith and his brother Hyrum were jailed in Carthage, Missouri, charged with starting a riot. On June 27, 1844, an angry mob stormed into the jail, removed the two brothers, and murdered them. The death of Joseph Smith paved the way for Brigham Young to become leader of the Mormon Church.

leaders spoke at an outdoor prayer meeting. When his turn came, Brigham's voice was filled with emotion. One woman cried out, "It is the voice of Joseph! It is Joseph Smith!" Many who were present agreed. Later that day, an assembly voted to let the Twelve run the church. Brigham was made church president.

Public pressure forced the state to cancel Nauvoo's city charter. For months, the city limped along without a legal government. With no police to keep order, Brigham buckled on a pair of six-shooters. He also took command of the Nauvoo Legion. Strangers who caused trouble were "sent to Aunt Peggy." That was Mormon slang for "giving them a whipping."

Clearly, the Mormons' days in Nauvoo were numbered. Brigham looked westward for a safe haven. He turned down Texas, Oregon, California, and Canada. Then he heard of the Great Salt Lake, which lay in a largely empty region called the Great Basin. With no other settlers nearby, the Mormons would be free to build their Promised Land.

Events were moving swiftly now. Smith's killers were tried, but the court found them not guilty. Roving mobs burned 150 Mormon houses. Brigham put his people to work building wagons for the trek west. By spring, he judged, there would be grass along the trail for the livestock. In December, federal marshals tried to arrest him on a false counterfeiting charge. Luckily, elder George Miller looked a lot like Brigham. Miller took his leader's place when the marshals came with their warrant. The trick left Brigham free to complete his plans.

On February 2, Brigham ordered his people to leave Nauvoo. Mormons sold their houses and farms for pennies on the dollar. One eight-thousand-dollar home brought only twelve dollars and fifty cents at auction. Two weeks later, Brigham led a wagon train into Iowa.

Chapter 5

The Promised Land

Today's Mormons look back on their exodus in biblical terms. Brigham was their Moses. Their new home in the Great Basin was the Promised Land. When a cold snap froze the Mississippi River, the Mormons pictured themselves crossing the Red Sea. During that cold winter, one hungry band of Mormons feasted on what seemed like a gift from heaven. The food came in the form of flocks of quail.

By May 1846, thousands of Mormons were rolling westward. They spread out across hundreds of miles of prairie. Brigham set up camps along the route. Farmers planted crops to feed those who would follow later. Kanesville grew up on the east bank of the Missouri River. On the west bank, a camp blossomed near what is now Omaha, Nebraska. The Mormons called it Winter Quarters.

In June, Captain James Allen rode into the Kanesville camp. The United States, he told Brigham, was at war with Mexico. He asked for a force of five hundred men to serve under General Stephen Kearny. Their task would be to help Kearny secure California for the Union. Brigham told Allen, "You shall have your Battalion, Sir." The act helped prove the church's loyalty. The $21,000 that the army paid to the men's families also factored into Brigham's decision.

Mormons looked up to Brigham as their religious leader. As the weeks passed, he proved his worth in other areas. As a builder, he pushed for the construction of log and sod houses. The crude dwellings sheltered nearly 3,500 people that winter. As a statesman, he made peace with the local American Indians. He also assured President James Polk that the Mormons were good Americans. As a leader, he could be stern. Men who broke the rules were whipped. But he also showed a softer side. To brighten the long days, he encouraged people to worship with music and dance.

Winter brought new hardships. Construction of much-needed wagons slowed to a snail's pace. Six hundred people died of illness and disease. Among the dead were two of Brigham's wives. Worn down by long, hard workdays, Brigham, too, fell ill.

Brigham Young needed a place where his people could live and worship freely. He solved the problem by picking an unsettled area in the Great Basin. The trek west was long and difficult. This illustration shows the Winter Quarters that Brigham set up near present-day Omaha, Nebraska.

In April 1847, healthy once more, Brigham led an advance party toward the Great Basin. The party included three women, two children, and 143 men. Each day started with a 5:00 A.M. wake-up call. After prayer and breakfast, the column moved out. All of the men carried rifles or pistols. At night, the men drew the wagons into a circle. By 9:00 P.M., all but the guards were asleep.

Pawnee war parties tracked the group. Brigham wooed them with gifts, but the warriors wanted more. One day, they set a prairie fire to frighten the Mormons. A wind shift drove the wall of flames away from the wagon train. When food supplies ran low, hunters spotted a herd of buffalo. That night, the women grilled buffalo steaks over buffalo chip fires.

At Fort Laramie, the Mormons picked up the Oregon Trail. The trail climbed through country that produced little grass. As supplies ran low, Brigham sent a crew ahead with a leather boat. The men ferried other settlers across the Platte River in return for food. The Mormons crossed the Platte on June 13. Ten days later, they sighted the Rocky Mountains.

The party had to endure dust, thin air, and a heavy workload. Many fell ill. Brigham was put to bed with Colorado tick fever. An advance party went ahead to blaze a trail. The main group followed. Brigham jolted along in the back of a wagon.

On July 21, the advance party let out a "shout of joy." Ahead lay the valley of the Great Salt Lake. Two days later, the men were plowing their first furrows. The sight of the "Promised Land" seemed to restore Brigham's strength. Newly energized, he plunged into the task of planning a new Zion.

Chapter 6

A Desert Valley Blossoms

With the new city taking shape, Brigham led a party back to Winter Quarters. Near South Pass, a Crow raiding party stole fifty horses. On a second eventful day, Brigham had to scramble to escape the claws of a grizzly bear. He met ten wagon trains of Mormons along the trail, all heading west. The great exodus was under way.

During the winter of 1847, Brigham took the title of prophet. As president and prophet, he now had complete control of the church. He also prepared his family for the move west. In May 1848, Brigham led a new column toward the Great Salt Lake. All but three of his wives made the 116-day journey. One of his wives, Louisa Beaman, gave birth to twin boys along the way.

When Brigham arrived that fall, much had changed. The Mexican War was over. The region was now part of the United States. More than five thousand settlers

Brigham Young speaks to his fellow Mormons at the Great Salt Lake. Once they reached that "Promised Land," the hard-working Mormons quickly built a thriving settlement.

lived in the valley. They had not been idle. Houses, mills, and irrigated fields gave proof of their labors.

The settlers had a wonderful tale to tell. That spring, swarms of hungry crickets had descended on their fields. Desperate men and women attacked the insects with brooms and torches. When that failed, they flooded the fields. For each cricket that drowned, two seemed to take its place. At that dark moment, flocks of seagulls flew in from the Great Salt Lake. In a short time, the birds snapped up most of the crickets.

Despite the miracle of the seagulls, food ran short that winter. By spring, the Mormons were eating tree bark, lily bulbs, and crows. Thanks to Brigham's rationing of food, no one starved. The California gold rush also helped. During 1849, many forty-niners passed through Salt Lake. The Mormons earned much-needed cash by repairing wagons and selling supplies. Brigham himself made $17,000 by trading with the gold seekers.

Brigham urged his people to make their own tools, harnesses, and cloth. He did not want them to depend on eastern factories. Brigham also worked to turn the vast region he called Deseret into a state. In Washington, D.C., his quest became tangled in the dispute over slavery. Should Deseret be slave or free? The North and South could not agree.

The Compromise of 1850 gave a short-lived answer. The bill set up a new and smaller Utah Territory. President Millard Fillmore named Brigham as governor. The new role gave Brigham a chance to develop Utah's resources. He urged Mormons to produce iron, lead, wool, and sugar beets. Held back by outdated methods, none of the projects was a long-term success.

Eager young Mormon missionaries traveled to Europe, Asia, and South Africa to preach their faith. In the 1850s, more converts headed west than the wagon trains could handle. From Iowa, many pushed handcarts across the 1,400-mile route. Some carts made of green wood fell apart. Disease and accidents thinned the ranks of the converts. Still, they trudged on. Brigham welcomed them with special warmth when they arrived. Utah needed people who were strong in body and faith.

In Salt Lake, the walls of a grand temple took shape. Nearby, Brigham built a large adobe house for his family. A coat of plaster gave the house its name—the White House. For a time, it served as family home, church headquarters, and territorial capitol. In 1855, Brigham built a new fourteen-room, two-story adobe house. Locals looked at its gilded tower and called it the Beehive House. It became Brigham's official residence.

The Mormon success story drew visitors from around the world. Among them were author Samuel Clemens (Mark Twain) and the British explorer Richard Burton. Newspaper editor Horace Greeley also dropped by. Greeley wrote that Brigham Young "carries the territory in his breeches pocket without a shadow of opposition." The New Yorker seemed to approve of the way his host used his power. Greeley described Brigham as modest, open, smart, and witty.

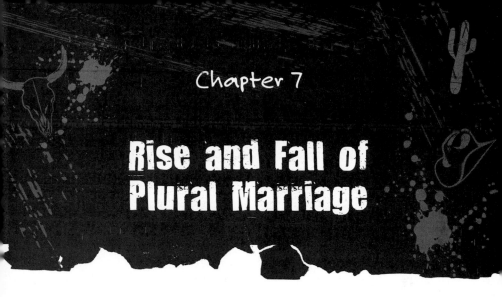

Chapter 7

Rise and Fall of Plural Marriage

S ome visitors came to Utah to watch the Mormons turn a desert into a garden. Others were drawn by a desire to see plural marriage in action. Rumors said that Brigham Young had ninety wives. Wasn't this a sinful way to live?

Church elders explained that "celestial marriage" was God's will. The doctrine had been revealed through Joseph Smith. Mormons, they added, did not invent polygamy. The Old Testament states that Abraham and Isaac each married more than one woman. In the Islamic faith, a man may have up to four wives. Closer to home, a number of American Indian tribes followed the practice.

The order to take more wives had shocked Brigham at first. His marriage to Mary Ann was a happy one. "[I]t was the first time in my life that I desired the grave," he said later. In time, Brigham put his duties to the church ahead of his feelings. He married his first plural wife when he was forty-one. In all, he married twenty-seven women, not ninety. Most were younger than he. A few were older widows. Five had been the wives of Joseph Smith. Brigham married these "caretaker wives" in order to protect them.

Brigham and his wives had fifty-seven children. Elizabeth, born in 1825, was the first. Mary, born in 1870, was the last. In the 1800s, many fathers enforced rules by whipping their children. Brigham was not one of them. To ensure that children came to prayers on time, he handed out small gifts. Clarissa Young Spencer remembered him as a wise, kind, and loving father. "The bond between my father and me was as close as if I had been his only child," she wrote. "I am sure that each of the other children felt the same way."

Brigham worked out a plan for housing his large family. Mary Ann, always a favorite, lived in Beehive House. As many as twelve wives and their children filled the nearby Lion House. The basement floor contained a schoolroom, laundry, dining room, and kitchen. Wives with younger children lived on the main floor. Older children and caretaker wives slept in

Brigham Young and his family walk to church in Salt Lake City. Over the years, he married twenty-seven women and fathered a family of fifty-seven children.

the top floor's twenty bedrooms. A prayer room on the main floor served double duty as a meeting room.

The wives divided the work. Lucy Decker managed the busy kitchen. Zina Huntington served as midwife and nurse. Other wives took charge of the washing, cleaning, and child care. Fifty people crowded around two long tables at mealtime. No one went hungry. Breakfast was eggs, milk, doughnuts, and stewed fruit. The five o'clock supper offered cornmeal mush, bread, fruit, and cheese. As a special treat, chicken was served at the midday meal on Sunday.

In the 1850s, the public assumed that all Mormons were polygamous. However, no more than 20 percent actually practiced plural marriage. Of this group, only 6 percent were married to five or more women. Money was one factor. Only wealthy Mormons could afford to keep up several homes filled with wives and children. Less-wealthy Mormons who felt compelled to practice celestial marriage often stopped with one extra wife.

As the years passed, outside pressures grew stronger. As long as Mormons practiced plural marriage, Utah could not become a state. Brigham also saw that many plural marriages were ending in divorce. In 1871, he softened the old rule: "A man," he said, "may embrace the law of celestial marriage in his heart and not take the second wife. . . ."

In 1890, long after Brigham's death, church president Wilford Woodruff took the final step. The Holy Spirit had spoken to him, he said. The church must conform to the law of the land. Except for a few stubborn holdouts, Mormons gave up the practice of polygamy.

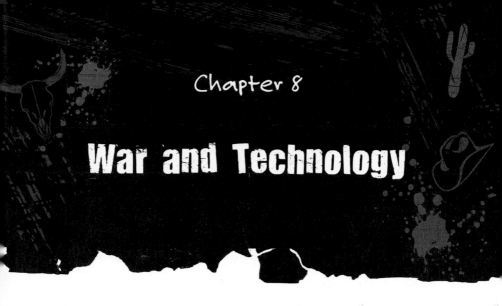

Chapter 8

War and Technology

The first shots of the Civil War were fired in 1861. Brigham refused to let Mormons fight for either side. "I am not an abolitionist or a pro-slavery man," he said. Joseph Smith, he noted, had once foretold the coming of such a war. The struggle, Brigham believed, would consume all nations. Only the Mormons would be spared.

President Abraham Lincoln let the Mormons go their own way. Fighting them would have strained the Union's resources, perhaps to the breaking point. "[T]ell Brigham Young," Lincoln said, "that if he will let me alone, I will let him alone."

Ever since the Utah War, army troops had been stationed in Utah. As the Civil War raged on, the soldiers withdrew. Brigham, with his keen eye for bargains, bought $1.6 million worth of surplus army gear for $40,000. He also renewed Utah's bid for statehood. He said, "[W]e [will] show our loyalty by trying to get in while others are trying to get out." The Mormons' foes in Congress blocked this effort, too.

In 1861, the government sliced off large chunks of the Utah Territory. A silver strike led to the birth of what is now Nevada. The gold rush region near Pike's Peak became part of Colorado. But Brigham did not object. He knew that non-Mormons would be drawn to those regions. Left to themselves, his people would be free to pursue their own way of life.

The Pony Express now was bringing news from the East in days, not weeks. Hard on the heels of the Pony Express riders came the telegraph. Brigham quickly grasped its value. His firm won the contract to install a thousand miles of telegraph lines. The first telegraph key chattered to life in his office at Beehive House in 1861. The Deseret Telegraph Company soon linked Mormon towns all over Utah.

Early in 1862, American Indian attacks threatened to close the Overland Trail. Brigham formed a mounted unit to keep the trail open. That summer, Colonel Patrick Connor arrived with 750 army troops. Connor hated Mormons, and he was determined to arrest Brigham. As an excuse, he cited a new federal law that

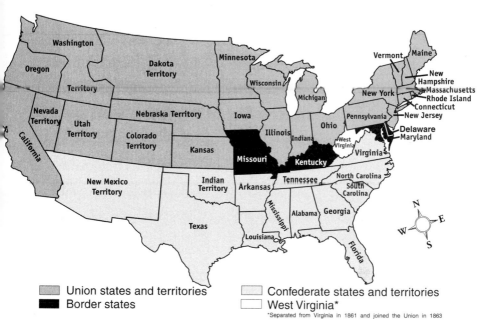

Union states and territories
Border states
Confederate states and territories
West Virginia*

*Separated from Virginia in 1861 and joined the Union in 1863

The Civil War divided the United States between the Union and the Confederacy, but Brigham Young and the Mormons chose to remain neutral. During the war, the U.S. government carved up the Utah Territory. This map shows how the nation was divided during the long and bitter war.

outlawed polygamy. As tensions built, armed Mormons kept watch on Beehive House. The sight of a raised flag would have called them to protect the prophet.

John Kinney, Utah's chief justice, found a way to outwit Connor. Kinney issued a court order that charged Brigham with breaking the anti-polygamy law. When Brigham appeared in court, Kinney set him free on bail. Then he postponed the trial again and again. The tactic robbed Connor of his excuse for arresting Brigham.

In 1864, Connor tried again. He accused Brigham of refusing to accept paper dollars as payment for supplies sold to the army. Brigham said he preferred banknotes backed by gold. This time General Irwin McDowell stepped in. He ordered Connor to back off. It was no time for the Union to go to war with the Mormons.

A new conflict began soon after the Civil War ended in 1865. Ute warriors struck the first blows by raiding Mormon settlements. It was an old story. Settlers were crowding onto land that belonged to the Ute. Because the army refused to help, Brigham had to organize a self-defense force. He also tried to make peace. However, Black Hawk, the Ute leader, turned him down. Over the next four years, Ute war parties drove the Mormons from twenty-five settlements. Only the Mormon's greater numbers forced Black Hawk to end the war.

By this time, the United States was working to link East and West by railroad. Brigham saw that the trains could transport converts quickly and safely. To multiply the benefits, he bid on the contract for laying track through Utah. The project brought much-needed paychecks to many Mormons.

Brigham lost his fight to route the tracks through Salt Lake City. The railroad chose a northern route through Ogden. Brigham fought back by building a railroad line from Salt Lake City to Ogden. Before long, work crews were laying track to all the major Mormon cities.

Chapter 9

"I Always Tried My Best"

B righam taught his people that Mormons must work together. Cooperation, he added, will accomplish more than any one person's labor. To pursue that goal, he promoted two plans. Merchants were asked to join the Zion Cooperative Mercantile Institution. When they did so, they turned over their goods to the cooperative. The church, in turn, asked members to avoid non-ZCMI merchants.

The second plan, known as the United Order, went further. In town after town, townsfolk bought shares in a local cooperative. Some co-ops grew crops such as cotton and flax. Others made products—shoes, brooms, hats, and leather goods. Members shared in the profits they earned. When United Order groups failed, it was for lack of capital, not effort.

Brigham often warned of the evils of tobacco and alcohol. He did not rule out all pleasures, however. In 1862, he opened the West's finest theater in Salt Lake City. With money scarce, playgoers paid for tickets with produce or eggs. Touring actors teamed with local Mormons to put on the plays. Brigham disliked plays filled with bad language and violence. In 1865, he banned the use of swear words on stage.

As with the theater, Brigham's feelings about women were mixed. On one hand, he thought a wife should be ruled by her husband. Men, he believed, are superior beings. Even so, he wanted Mormon women to be well schooled. Brigham pointed them toward jobs in offices, banks, and stores. He also urged women to study law and medicine. The first class of the University of Deseret reflected his views. The school enrolled 223 students in 1868. Of these, 103 were women.

Brigham's word was law to most of his wives. That was not the case with Ann Eliza Webb. In 1875, Ann Eliza sued Brigham for divorce on grounds of neglect. The case was heard by one of Brigham's foes, Judge James McKean. McKean awarded Ann Eliza with an alimony settlement of five hundred dollars a month. When Brigham refused to pay, McKean held him in

As he aged, Brigham Young's health began to fail. He was forced to live part-time in southern Utah to avoid Salt Lake City's frigid winters. Vigorous to the end, the courageous Mormon leader died on August 29, 1878.

contempt of court. He set the fine at twenty-five dollars, plus a day in jail. On March 11, the seventy-three-year-old Mormon leader served his sentence. The divorce itself dragged on and on. In 1877, a second judge threw the case out of court. Brigham and Ann Eliza, he ruled, had never been legally married.

As he aged, Brigham was hobbled by rheumatism. In winter, he fled the chill of Salt Lake City for the milder climate of southern Utah. A case of mumps sent him to bed in 1870. An enlarged prostate caused him more misery. Brigham sometimes said he looked forward to being reborn. In heaven, he joked, he would have new teeth and perfect eyesight.

The end came suddenly. On August 23, 1878, he fell ill with violent cramps. Doctors told him he had a form of cholera. Modern doctors believe that his appendix had burst. Brigham held on for six days. The end came on August 29. As he died, he cried out, "Joseph! Joseph! Joseph!" Those who heard him believe he was greeting Joseph Smith.

Thousands of mourners filed past his casket as it lay in the Tabernacle. They came to say good-bye to a legend of the Wild West. Many called him an American Moses. Like the biblical Moses, he had led his people to a Promised Land. Under his leadership, the Mormon Church had grown strong and prosperous.

Historian Wallace Stegner called Brigham "a colonizer without equal in the history of America. In a desert that nobody wanted . . . he planted . . . over three hundred and fifty towns. . . . " He was both loved and hated, but no one doubted his courage and resolve. As Brigham himself wrote, "I was so gritty that I always tried my best."

Glossary

abolitionist—Someone who worked to abolish slavery in the years before the Civil War.

Apostles; the Twelve—In the Mormon church, the twelve high-ranking members of the administrative council.

apprentice—A trainee who learns a trade by working under the supervision of an experienced craftsperson.

bail—Money that people accused of crimes post with a court to ensure their appearance for trial.

bloc voting—A group of voters who agree to support a slate of candidates or legislative proposals.

celestial marriage—The Mormon Church's name for plural marriage or polygamy.

cholera—An acute infectious disease of the small intestine.

city charter—A permit issued by a state that allows a town or city to create its own local government.

Civil War—The war between the Union, the northern states, and the Confederacy, the southern states, 1861–1865.

contempt of court—A legal term applied to someone who insults a court or refuses to obey a judge's orders.

converts—People who have been persuaded to adopt a particular religion.

cooperative—An enterprise that is owned or managed jointly by those who use its facilities or services.

elder—One of the officers of a church, often having minister-like or teaching duties. In the Mormon Church, an elder is a member of the higher order of priesthood.

exodus—The movement of a large number of people from one homeland to another.

Forty-Niners—The men and women who took part in the 1849 California gold rush.

militia—Part-time soldiers who are called to duty in times of emergency.

Mormon Tabernacle—One of the church's historic meeting halls, located on Temple Square in Salt Lake City.

pardon—The act by a president or governor that grants legal forgiveness for a crime.

plural marriage; polygamy—The practice of having more than one spouse at a time.

Pony Express—An overland mail service (1860–1861) that relied on relays of riders and horses to carry the mail.

prairie—A treeless region of flat or rolling grasslands.

tuberculosis—A deadly bacterial disease that most often affects the lungs. In Brigham Young's time, the disease was known as consumption.

wildcat bank—A bank that conducts business even though it does not have a state charter.

Zion—An ideal community or society that lives in harmony and devotes itself to serving God.

Further Reading

Books

Bial, Raymond. *Nauvoo: Mormon City on the Mississippi River.* Boston: Houghton Mifflin, 2006.

Ching, Jacqueline. *Utah: Past and Present.* New York: Rosen Central, 2011.

Domnauer, Teresa. *Westward Expansion.* New York: Children's Press, 2010.

Gunderson, Cory Gideon. *Brigham Young: Pioneer and Prophet.* Mankato, Minn.: Bridgestone Books, 2003.

Sonneborn, Liz. *The Mormon Trail.* New York: Franklin Watts, 2005.

Internet Addresses

Brigham Young Biography
<http://unicomm.byu.edu/about/brigham.aspx>

PBS—New Perspectives on the West: Brigham Young
<http://www.pbs.org/weta/thewest/people/s_z/young.htm>

Utah History to Go: Brigham Young
<http://historytogo.utah.gov/people/brighamyoung.html>

Index